# Invisible Currents

## Nature's Lessons
## for the Mind and Heart

# Invisible Currents

## Nature's Lessons
## for the Mind and Heart

by
Wanda McGee

with illustrations by
Cindy Mueller

Miles River Press

## Acknowledgments

I would like to thank those whose valuable and appreciated help made this book possible: Cindy Mueller, whose magnificent artwork is as important as the words; Linda Harteker, a respected editor and friend; Peg Paul, an insightful editor and publisher; and Sheila Gibson, Peg's talented assistant. Also, those who encouraged me when I needed it the most: Delores Allegra, Ed Briggs, Bill McGee, Judy Metcalf, Shirley Miekka, Donna Peratino, Kathy and Joe Schwar, Jeff Shenot, Hilda Spain-Owen, Lisa Stevens, B.J. Stober, and Ruth Upchurch. And finally, a heartfelt thanks to all members of my family for their enduring encouragement and support.

Wanda McGee<br>January 2000

*Published by*
Miles River Press
400 Madison Street, #1309
Alexandria, Virginia  22314
(800) 767-1501
www.milesriverpress.com

Book and Cover Design by
Donna J. Dove, K&D Limited, Inc.

Library of Congress Cataloging-in-Publication Data

McGee, Wanda 1939-
  Invisible currents : nature's lessons for the mind and heart / by Wanda McGee ; with illustrations by Cindy Mueller.
    p.   cm
  ISBN 0-917917-13-8 (alk. paper)
  1. Conduct of life. 2. Nature--Psychological aspects. 3. Chesapeake and Ohio Canal (Md. and Washington, D.C.)--Miscellanea. I. Title.

BF637.C5 M37 1999
158.1'28--dc21                                        99-050201

# Table of Contents

# Preface

In this world of rapid change, where friends and relatives are often far away, we tend to scatter ourselves and our time. We end up feeling disconnected. Nature can bring us home again — where we remember who we are and what really matters. Wherever there is a wild place, there, just for the noticing, is a gift of love and strength we can give to ourselves.

The Chesapeake & Ohio Canal is such a place for me. This book is based on more than 25 years of walking, looking, listening, and learning, along the C&O Canal. It could just as easily have been set among the wheat fields of Kansas, the mountains of Austria, the outback of Australia, or any one of thousands of beautiful wild places on this planet.

The Chesapeake & Ohio Canal entered my life in the sultry early summer of 1973 when I moved to a small community in Maryland, just outside our nation's capital. Over the years, the canal became a good friend — ever changing, yet a source of constant delight. Rich in the unexpected and always there, it was supportive and comforting during life's bad times and a source of joy and delight during the good.

My relationship with the C&O Canal was the glue that held me in place during periods of financial insecurity and personal turmoil. The stress of a divorce in the mid-1970s and of two teenaged sons evolving into manhood in the 1980s was eased as the landscape slid by during walks and runs on the towpath. In time, the challenges of my personal life brought a deep attachment to the narrow canal, its rustic locks, and its canal houses. At the same time, life was serving up a new set of challenges as a graduate degree acted as my bridge to the world of business management. I moved my meditations upstream to deep, still waters and made a place in my heart and my life for learning the lessons the Widewater area of the canal had to teach.

Widewater, a small section of the long (184.5 miles) canal, is located between Old Angler's Inn and Great Falls Tavern Visitor Center in the C&O National Historical Park in Potomac, Maryland. This park, one of the most visited national parks in the U.S., is a complex natural organization. It held the key to my search for answers in the equally complex, and sometimes painful, world of business. As questions or challenges arose in business life, answers unfailingly came during a long walk along the canal. The answer was in the form of something noticed and pondered upon—a great blue heron blending into a rock, a single flower blooming along the trail, green algae covering a pond. Observations of natural phenomena and questions of how they related to some aspect of life were the doorways to exploring both internal and external landscapes.

My hope in writing this book is to share with readers some of the gifts the canal has so generously given. These gifts, in the form of simple stories, accompanied by questions for contemplation and dialogue, are offered as a way to move the quality of communication forward in the lives of individuals and organizations. Throughout this book, when you see the word "organization," please take it to mean any group or relationship in which you are involved, such as family, church, club, business, and, perhaps most important, your relationship with yourself. I trust you will not find "answers" in the pages of this book.

My best hope is that you find events in nature you can relate to, and questions you can think and talk about to find your own answers. May you be blessed in your ability to use natural places, wherever you are, as a source of steady sustenance and to support yourself through life's dilemmas.

Wanda McGee
January 2000

# Spring

If you're going to take a risk,
be sure to have support behind you.

# Standing Watch

A small flock of mallards is feeding in
the shallow water along the canal banks.
The green heads of the males flash,
iridescent in the afternoon light. As they
look for food, members of the flock take
turns searching and watching. While the
searching ducks plunge their heads into the
water, their tails go up. The watching
ducks stay alert, ready to signal danger.

## Points to Ponder . . .

Has someone ever stood watch for you in a way that allowed you
to look beneath the surface during a critical time in your life?
What were the results?

Have you stood such a watch for someone else? If so, how?

What do you find helpful when someone is supporting you in
creating your own beneficial change? What is not helpful?

How could you use these insights to help yourself and others deal
with life's transitions?

Slowing the pace reveals many
treasures to identify and enjoy.

# Slowing Down

Visitors going to Great Falls Overlook cross Olmsted Island on a meandering walkway. They walk briskly on high bridges that cross ravines where rushing water zigzags around trees and massive, craggy boulders. As these visitors scurry along, looking at the next bend in the planked path, very few notice the details of this rare and fragile ecosystem. Small, delicate flowers perch precariously on island rocks. Pink and white hepatica blossoms, seasonal gifts on slender stems, await recognition by those who slow down enough to search them out. Most hikers, intent on reaching the Overlook, miss these briefly blooming treasures.

*Points to Ponder . . .*

What do you notice when you slow down? What do you miss when you don't?

What are the gifts in your life that are here for only a short time? In what ways do you acknowledge them? Ignore them?

What might happen if you balanced your attention between life's passing gifts and its more showy attractions?

How could paying attention to life's passing gifts be used to strengthen your family? Your organization?

Natural gifts abound when we truly
open ourselves to seeing them.

# Natural Gifts

Between Widewater and Old Angler's Inn, there is an eye-catching cliff with an impressionistic splash of color across its face. Its design has evolved over the decades since the canal was built. The natural canvas, a sheer rock face, extends about 20 feet above the water line. It is slate-gray, painted over with yellow-green lichen. The contemporary design blends perfectly with the surrounding earth tones. The still water of the canal reflects the rock face, doubling the effect of this natural work of art.

*Points to ponder . . .*

When you recall moments of real beauty in your life, what images come to mind?

During those experiences, in what way were you transformed? How does this effect continue?

How can you use awareness of your own and others' natural gifts to increase your effectiveness in the world?

Each stage of development is unique and
important to the overall life cycle.

# Growth Stages

Wildflowers of many colors, sizes, and shapes grow along the canal. They are everywhere — in shade, sun, rocky hillsides, damp gullies, and fertile meadows. Some are newly in bloom, with a few full blossoms and many buds. Some, more mature, have many blossoms and few buds. Still others have wilted flowers and are forming seeds.

*Points to ponder . . .*

How does the life cycle of wildflowers remind you of the dynamics of a group over time?

In your experience, what makes a group successful? What part does diversity play?

What appear to be the underlying reasons for group success?

What are your ideas for recognizing and supporting groups in an organization as they evolve over time? How would you support the talents of individuals in the groups?

As groups evolve over time, how could you and your organization best recognize and support the gifts of their seasons?

When there is competition,
someone is bound to lose.

# Competition

A female duck is picking a partner.
First, she flies with one competitor, then
the other. Sometimes, both pursue her at
the same time. She alights on the water
briefly between flights. All three ducks
quack loudly, intermittently. She won't let
either suitor get too close to her. Finally,
she makes her decision, and the pair flies
away. Having done his best, the rejected
duck settles on the water to shake out and
preen his feathers in the afternoon sun.

*Points to ponder . . .*

What is your attitude toward winning? Losing?

Have you ever won and felt like you lost? Lost, and felt like you won?

When you are competing with another organization (or within your own organization) and the outcome is beyond your control, how can you improve your chances of success?

What are possible alternatives to unnecessary competition in your life?

How could each alternative benefit you? Your relationships? Your organization?

A positive environment
encourages gradual growth.

# Gradual Growth

A black-water pool on the side of the towpath opposite the canal mirrors bits and pieces of a slate-gray sky. It is a beautiful, disorderly place. New leaves, broken off by the recent wind and rain, add bits of bright color and contrast with the dark depths of the pool. Clusters of wild blue-purple irises, unusual in the pools along this part of the canal, send eager young stalks skyward. Over the years, the irises have multiplied in friendly places along the boundary of the pool.

*Points to Ponder . . .*

How would you describe a positive environment?

What part of yourself do you suppress because there is no friendly environment for it? What would it take to change this?

How might you nurture individual growth within your family? Your organization?

When there is a filter, directness is lost.

# Directness

After a heavy morning downpour, the weather has cleared. Widewater's surface is a liquid mirror, reflecting the new green of spring, anchored by the gray of shoreline rocks. Although a whispering breeze ruffles the tops of the trees, no ripples stir the quiet water. There, where a large elm tree hangs over the canal, a raindrop pattern shows clearly on the still surface. This giant umbrella is still shedding its watery mantle.

*Points to ponder . . .*

Today's information overload has been likened to a rainstorm. How do you experience this in your life? How at work?

What information comes straight from its original source? What is filtered in some way?

What kind of information do you feel is most useful? Most frustrating? Most fun? Most thought-provoking? Most life-enhancing?

In your experience, what promotes the flow of information throughout an organization? What happens when there is limited information? An adequate amount? An excessive amount?

How can you use the flood of information in today's world to increase your knowledge base at home and at work without creating confusion?

With synergy, the whole becomes greater than
the sum of the parts.

# Synergy

In the summerlike heat of the late
May afternoon, a light breeze disperses
the gnats. At first, the air seems deserted,
except for small birds that occasionally flit
in and out of low bushes. Then soft hoots
of unseen owls, deep in the woods, begin to
float on the warm breeze, perfumed by
honeysuckle. In the sky, buzzards coast in
slow-moving spirals, riding easily on
invisible currents of air below high, white
fluffy clouds.

*Points to ponder . . .*

How have you experienced synergy in your life?

What was purposeful about that time? What happened
accidentally?

If you were in charge of a project that needed everyone's best
effort to succeed, how would you create the necessary
synergy?

Given time after a setback,
new growth can come forth.

# Hidden Strength

A tree stump, sawed off a few feet above the ground and presumed dead, is expressing the miracle of renewal. Its roots, stewards of the tree's energy during the barren winter, have redirected their life-supporting sap outward. Strong green shoots at the base of the stump hold the promise of continued life.

*Points to Ponder . . .*

What do you remember about an unwanted change in your life that you eventually handled well? How did you manage it?

When did you know that you were recovering from the disaster and that new growth was occurring?

What value from this experience can you draw on to handle future change?

Where in your personal and organizational life would you like to nurture new growth? How could you go about doing this?

Transitions are so gradual that it's hard to tell
where one stage ends and another begins.

# Transitions

On Widewater in late afternoon,
patches of light glint on gently rippling
water. Leaves and heavy pollen float in a
protected place. In the distance, two ducks
paddle leisurely about, searching for food.
The water overflow, that in early spring
gurgled with the abundance of high water,
is now silent. Trees are in full leaf.
Widewater, poised for summer, is tranquil
and still. A person who did not know it is
spring might guess it is already July.

## Points to Ponder . . .

In the cycles of life, what seem to be the qualities that are the
equivalent of spring and summer seasons?

What are the signs that you are moving from spring to summer in
some part of your life (perhaps a job, a relationship) or in the
overall life cycle itself?

Thinking of your organization, what are the signs that a transition
is occurring?

What do these two seasons contribute to the lives of individuals
and organizations? How is it possible to make the most of
them?

# Summer

BICYCLE DETOUR
ROCKY AREA
AHEAD

When choosing a path, consider both the
information and the options.

# Choices

Below Great Falls Tavern Visitor
Center, just after Lock 15, the towpath
becomes a mass of jumbled stones and
boulders. Bicycle riders have a choice of
detouring around this area or carrying their
bikes across the tortuous and sometimes
slippery transit. Their point of decision is
at the bottom of a wooden staircase leading to a canal footbridge between Locks 16
and 17. It comes well before they can see
the rocks ahead. Those who carry their
bikes up the stairs have an easy ride
through quiet woods. Those who continue
on the towpath, next to the water, face the
challenge of the unseen rocks ahead.

*Points to ponder . . .*

What is the difference between a decision and a choice?

How does having a say about where you are going influence your
commitment to getting there? To accepting what happens
along the way?

When has your organization been faced with a difficult choice?
How was the decision made? Who decided? What happened
to you?

What decision-making processes do you use? How about the
people around you? How do these processes include or
exclude "the people who will be carrying the bikes?"

What could you do to make your decision-making processes
more inclusive? How about the decisions someone else
makes that still affect you?

Standing out doesn't mean
standing alone.

# Standing Out

Many small footpaths connect overlooks along the Potomac River with the canal towpath. Along one of these footpaths, a single flower—a wild phlox on a tall stem—stands. It seems to be alone, rooted to its spot. There is nothing like it nearby. A variety of plants, surrounds this purple bloom; they are equally appealing, but not so noticeable.

*Points to Ponder . . .*

Who or what in your life and your organization claims the spotlight of attention? Supports those in the spotlight without claiming notice?

How does each serve the other?

What are the advantages and disadvantages of being a stand out? A less showy part of the whole?

How could these different styles better support one another?

Where is your place in this landscape? Where would you like it to be? What would be your first step in getting there?

It takes many diverse voices
to make a full chorus.

# Diversity

A fresh morning follows a late-night rainfall. In a blend of spontaneous voices, birds welcome the new day. Their many songs create a chorus. All sound bright and enthusiastic. While each bird sings in its own full-throated voice and has its own unique song, there is harmony in this diversity.

*Points to Ponder . . .*

What does diversity mean to you?

What important part does diversity play in your life? What part does it play in the culture of your organization?

In what ways is it easy to recognize and appreciate diversity? In what ways is it difficult?

How can diversity be a unifying factor in an organization?

What happens today, even the small
events, determines future directions.

# Awareness

Wild irises stand out boldly in the receding waters of what, in spring, was a black-water pool. Only two of the once abundant blue-purple blossoms remain. Now withered and dull, they are almost hidden by spikes of green foliage. The delicate mystery of the black-water pool is gone. Summer's heavy pollen covers the water's surface. On the bottom of the shallow pool, fallen leaves are accumulating. They will feed next year's foliage. Occasionally, a leaf alights on the water's surface. It briefly floats and then spirals downward.

*Points to ponder . . .*

What seemingly small events in your life – like single leaves spiraling into the water – were more significant than they seemed at the time?

Looking at these events as a whole, what seems to be their pattern?

What have they taught you about life? What about them inspires learning?

How might you use what you have learned to nurture your personal growth? The growth of your organization?

Open space provides breathing room for both
survival and celebration.

# Breathing Space

Widewater's vibrancy and openness
welcome visitors and inhabitants alike.
Hikers, bikers, dogs, and geese make room
for one another as they go about their
lives. A mallard family, swimming next
to a small island, shares the water's
sparkling surface with a red canoe. A
small group picnics in a shady place.
Sounds of the moment float over the open
water. As the towpath curves along
Widewater, it provides an unobstructed
view of water, sky, rocks, and trees.

*Points to Ponder . . .*

What does personal breathing space mean to you?

What about your life and the life of your organization is open and
unobstructed and gives you breathing space? What seems to
close you in?

What part do play and celebration have in your own survival?
How might this be applied to the life of an organization?

How can you create openness and breathing space in your life?
In your organization?

The possibility of negative results
can create strong boundaries.

# Boundaries

In some places on the well-traveled
towpath, the earth is packed so hard that
it sheds the rain. Along one such stretch,
poison ivy spreads profusely. It covers the
canal bank, from the water right up to the
path. Dressed in the dark green of summer,
the plant's three-leaf clusters are easy to
recognize. Along this stretch, no anglers
have slid down the bank to fish. There is
not even one set of footprints off the path.

*Points to Ponder . . .*

How have your life experiences (such as culture, age, education,
profession) shaped your beliefs about boundaries? How do
you feel about this?

What are the natural boundaries that seem to limit your personal
path? Which ones were put in place by you? By someone
else?

Where in your life do you find the most limiting boundaries?
Those most open to passage?

What are the advantages of both positive and negative boundaries
in your life? What are the disadvantages?

How does your thinking about boundaries apply to organizational
life?

Even though underlying structures
seem immovable, they change over
time.

# Foundations

Hundreds of thousands of gallons of water surge over Great Falls every minute. In its downstream rush over the distance of two hundred yards, the roaring Potomac River falls the same height as a four-story building. While the amount of water pouring over the rocks changes throughout the year, the underlying structure of Mather Gorge remains much the same over time. However, riverbed rocks, most visible during the low water of late summer, do change slowly over the eons.

*Points to Ponder . . .*

What about your life, and the life of your organization, reminds you of river bedrock? The flow of water over the falls?

How do the underlying structure—the bedrock— and the water flow influence each other?

If you could alter either the underlying structure or the flow of your life or work, what would be different?

What prevents you from taking action?

The appearance of strength is
sometimes deceiving.

# Inner Secret

A healthy-looking tree, toppled across the towpath in a recent storm, has blocked the progress of hikers and bicyclists for a few days. Now, workers clearing the path have removed a section of the tree. A clean chain-saw cut exposes a cross-section of the trunk. The center is rotten. Great gaping holes inside the tree left it unable to support itself in the whipping wind.

## Points to Ponder . . .

What image do you associate with inner strength? What tests its integrity?

What do you remember about a time in your life when you appeared strong yet felt unstable at your core? When you appeared weak yet were really strong?

What brought you through these difficult times?

If you were asked how individuals and organizations can maintain a solid core during the uncertainties of life, what would you say?

Without foresight and planning,
dealing with challenges can be
extremely difficult.

# Looking Ahead

The Billy Goat Trail begins just below Great Falls and makes a scenic detour around Widewater. The outside loop of this hiking trail swings away from the canal, just above Lock 16, then follows a rocky ridge along the Potomac River above Mather Gorge, and rejoins the towpath at the lower end of Widewater. In the heat of summer, the trail is especially challenging to those without hiking boots, drinking water, and the necessary agility.

## Points to Ponder . . .

Have you ever faced a life challenge for which you weren't prepared? If so, what happened? In what ways could you have better prepared yourself?

What is the biggest challenge you face in the next few months in your life? In your organization?

When the challenge is met, how will you know you have succeeded?

In what ways are you prepared? For instance, what physical resources, experience, human support do you have?

In addition to what you already have, what else do you need in order to achieve success? How might you obtain what you need?

Chaos in the creative process can
still produce success.

# Unexpected Results

Throughout the summer, green algae have steadily grown on the surface of a still, small pond adjacent to the Widewater towpath. The first algae, unnoticed on the water's surface, multiplied to form small, slippery-looking clumps. They grew larger and now cover the entire surface of the pool. The summer-long process has produced a velvety green blanket.

## Points to Ponder . . .

In what ways do the algae and the pond remind you of your life and the life of your organization?

Have you ever worked on something that started small, was rather chaotic, and eventually produced unexpected results? How did this happen?

Have you worked on something that followed an orderly, controlled process only to result in a mess? If so, what seemed to prevent the desired outcome?

How is it possible to balance our human need for order and control with our acceptance of the unplanned?

Autumn

When pileups occur,
energy eventually causes movement.

# Moving Beyond

A quarter-mile downstream from Widewater, opposite Old Angler's Inn, a trail leading to the towpath crosses a canal culvert. On its upstream side, the junk of summer — floating in the low water of autumn — cannot move downstream. It dams the opening of the large drainpipe. Dead branches catch and trap all sorts of debris. It's an ugly mess. Still, the moving water easily finds its way through to the other side of the culvert where now it flows freely.

*Points to Ponder . . .*

In what ways do the water and the clogged culvert remind you of life?

What piles up in organizations? What makes it collect? What purpose does it serve?

How is the debris you encounter in organizational life similar to what you experience in your personal life? How is it different?

What can be gained from getting rid of personal and organizational junk? What are the benefits and risks of doing it quickly?

What are your options for encouraging an easy flow in your life?

Places that seem isolated and apart are really
connected to the larger world.

# Connected

On a quiet weekday afternoon, it is easy for hikers along Widewater to imagine themselves far away from the large metropolitan area. This time of year, the water is framed by colorful hardwood trees and dark cedars. Rocky shores and small islands add to the effect. Although this place of refuge seems remote, the roar of airplanes frequently interrupts the canal's tranquillity. As they follow a flight path to a major airport, the planes are a constant reminder that Widewater is connected to the larger world.

*Points to Ponder . . .*

If you were to draw a map showing connections in your life, what would it look like? Would it include family members, friends, work associates, organizations, nature, spirit?

How are these connections related? Which are visible? Invisible? Which connections are strongest? Weakest?

Ideally, how would you like these connections to be? If you decided to change them in some way, what would be your first step?

Clear reflection calls for calm stillness.

# Reflection

On a still autumn day, fiery yellows,
oranges, and reds surround the glassy
reflection of a white lockhouse at water's
edge. The image of the lockhouse and the
gray branches of an overhanging tree stay
much the same, even as the colors around
them change. But that mirror image can
change in a moment—if the wind gusts or
a fish jumps.

*Points to Ponder . . .*

What role does reflection play in your life? How does it occur in
your organization?

Under what conditions do you best learn from experience? How
do you reflect on and learn from your mistakes?

How could you use times of reflection to help create a more vital
existence for yourself? For your organization?

How might you achieve a better balance between action and
reflection? How could this help your family or organization?

It takes time and patience to fully understand
and appreciate some of life's experiences.

# Ripening

Persimmons, about the size of plums,
are an inviting golden yellow, but not yet ripe
in early autumn. When an unsuspecting
hiker tries a bite, puckered lips and a wide
grimace quickly follow. Only after a frost
are the persimmons, now orange and
beginning to wrinkle, sweet and edible.

*Points to Ponder . . .*

How do you usually react when confronted by something
different or unfamiliar?

Can you think of something in your life that you didn't like at first,
but later accepted, maybe even enjoyed?

How have you noticed this happening in organizations?
What seems to be at the heart of this effect?

What in your life, or the life of your organization, seems to need
a time of ripening? How could you create the space to allow
this to happen?

Obstacles can become assets when we recognize
and design around them.

# Obstacles

The path to Great Falls Overlook is designed to be accessible to everyone. Concrete footbridges cross rocky gorges and rushing water. Informational plaques are posted along boardwalks. In some places, large rocks have been made part of the structure of the walkways, helping to determine design and direction. These natural obstacles add beauty to the path.

*Points to Ponder . . .*

What are the biggest obstacles you have dealt with in the past? How did you design around them?

How did you react when the obstacles were expected? When they were unexpected? When they were personal? When they were organizational?

In what ways were you successful or unsuccessful in dealing with these obstacles? How have these experiences become assets in your life?

In handling future obstacles, what do you hope to do differently?

A compelling vision can motivate us
to take a closer look.

# Strong Attraction

On the canal towpath, just below
Great Falls Tavern Visitor Center, hikers
stop to gaze toward the Potomac River. In
the late afternoon sunlight, they catch a
distant glimpse of a sandy beach and
sparkling water. Even though the beach is
now deserted, footprints in the sand
leading to the water show that many were
drawn off the towpath in order to get a
wider view.

## Points to Ponder . . .

When you think about motivation, what draws you in? What is
the source of the appeal?

Once you have become initially interested, what determines
whether you make a commitment to action and follow
through on it?

Regardless of whether you consider yourself a leader, what could
you do in your organization to help create an environment
that motivates people to become involved and even
committed?

As time passes, stark reminders of mistakes
are easy to see and identify.

# Mistakes

Unexpected spots of color dance on
the surface of a small pool near the concrete
footbridge at Widewater. Four fishing
bobbers in three color combinations — red
and white, orange and white, and yellow-
ish-green and white — are strung on fine
lines entangled in small, bare branches.
They are continuing reminders of failed
attempts to hook a prize.

*Points to Ponder . . .*

What prizes do you personally fish for in life? In your
organization, what do people seem to value most?

What happens when a person or team does its best to hook a
prize and doesn't succeed?

Does reaction to a failed attempt seem to vary depending on
where an organization or project is in its lifecycle? If so,
how?

In what ways can failed attempts be positive experiences?

In your organization, what would it take for failed attempts to be
treated consistently as learning opportunities?

Intrusive observation can cause those
on the receiving end to take flight.

# Observation

In the dim light of late afternoon, a
great blue heron — hunched on a slate-gray
boulder not more than 30 feet away — is
unnoticed until he moves slightly. As
hikers stop to admire the big bird, they
gesture toward him and talk quietly and
excitedly. The heron quickly tires of the
scrutiny and, with a deep rasping croak,
spreads ample wings in flight.

*Points to ponder . . .*

What does observation mean to you?

In the past, when your performance or behavior was being
observed, under what circumstances did you do your best?
Your worst?

What part did feedback play in this process? How was it
beneficial? In what way did it make you want to take flight?

If your colleagues asked you to observe their performance and
give them feedback, how would you do it? How would you
want them to do it for you?

We hear a lot better
when our own noise stops.

# Listening

On a sunny fall day, gravel and crisp brown leaves crunch and rustle underfoot. A faint, sharp sound, filtered through the noise of footsteps on the path, is unrecognizable. However, when the crunch and rustle stop, not one sound, but many, rush in to fill the silence. Now it is easy to identify the shrill cry as that of a blue jay. On the other side of Widewater, a spring-fed stream gurgles down a hillside and into the canal. Dry leaves clinging to an oak tree rustle in the wind. In the distance, crows caw.

*Points to Ponder . . .*

What personal noises and filters prevent you from listening to others? To yourself?

What about others makes it difficult for you to listen to them?

How do the collective noises and filters of you and your colleagues influence your ability to work together?

How could you stop your own noise and listen more effectively?

Anticipating predictable change
allows time for planning.

# Planning Ahead

The canal at historic Great Falls
Tavern is the summer mooring place of a
replica of a nineteenth-century canal boat.
It is used to educate and entertain visitors
during the warm weather. They board the
boat for a mule-drawn ride through a short
portion of the canal. Now, in autumn, its
wooden hull rests on sturdy blocks instead
of buoyant waves. In preparation for
winter, the locks have been drained. The
boat is still there.

*Points to Ponder . . .*

When have you experienced a season of hardship in your life?
In what ways was it predictable? Unpredictable?

Could better planning have helped you move through this
season? How so?

In the future, what might be the signs that a hard time is
approaching? What valuable resource would you want to
protect during that time? How would you go about doing it?

# Winter

Adapting to the circumstances of our
environment makes survival possible.

# Adapting

A small tree, stripped bare in winter, embraces without touching the curved face of a large rounded boulder. Its sinuous shape shows its determination to reach the light — and to survive. Farther along the path, a tree growing next to a sheer, perpendicular rock face grows straight and tall. Although its objective of survival is the same, its shape, determined by its circumstances, is different.

*Points to Ponder . . .*

In the context of organizational life, what does it mean to adapt?

Have you ever experienced a situation in an organization where you needed to adapt in order to survive? What happened?

How can you use the lessons of your own adaptation to influence what is new and evolving in your organization?

What does this adaptation mean in terms of your personal life?

The character of our work becomes
more apparent as time passes.

# Lasting Value

In crisp early December at Widewater, the blue cloudless sky is reflected in wide sweeps across the water. Now it is easy to notice a bird's nest mirrored in the canal. Crafted in a high fork of a maple tree and secured by surrounding branches, the nest is cone shaped. Unlike a mourning dove's nest, which disintegrates almost before the young leave it, this nest has been designed to weather the winter ahead.

*Points to Ponder . . .*

What are you carefully crafting in your life that you hope will be lasting?

What would you say if someone asked you to describe the value you are adding to your organization?

What prevents you from giving full value to your work daily?

How is it possible to clear what is getting in the way of your consistently achieving excellence?

A single event can mean
different things to different people.

# Perceptions

A foot of powdery snow, fallen from a windless nighttime sky, has stopped traffic on local roads. Motorists who feel the need to venture out before the snowplow comes face hazardous conditions. By contrast, skiers who live near the canal appreciate a rare opportunity to use the towpath as a cross-country track. The soft snow muffles the joyous voices of people of all ages, sizes, and abilities, as they stride and glide with varying amounts of ease and grace

*Points to Ponder . . .*

How do winter storms remind you of life?

In what ways have you experienced life's storms as destructive? Constructive?

What might happen if you consistently looked at these storms as opportunities instead of disasters?

How can you apply these insights as you participate in the life of your organization?

Rigid barriers test even the
most dedicated persistence.

# Persistence

It is a cold, winter afternoon. A large
fish lies lifeless under transparent ice.
Attempting to reach the fish, a hungry
crow alternately pecks the ice and squawks
its frustration. Noisy members of its
extended family gather in the surrounding
trees. The ruckus increases as two of the
birds take turns swooping down upon the
one on the ice. When a bald eagle and two
herons fly low to check out the activity, the
crows scatter. Soon, a lone crow returns
and continues its work—silently.

*Points to ponder . . .*

What comes to mind when you think about barriers to success in
your life? Are they sometimes invisible?

How do the people around you contribute to those barriers? How
do they provide the support needed to move through them?

What is your part in this process? Do you see yourself as a victim
of circumstances or as someone who prevails in spite of
setbacks?

When faced with barriers in the past, what has enabled you and
others to persist and succeed? How do you know when to
keep going and when to stop?

If we intend to move forward, the journey
continues, no matter what the conditions.

# Journeying

During a midwinter thaw, the snow
on the towpath has turned to slush.
Footprints, filled with water, clearly mark
the forward direction of a hiker's journey.
Sometimes, the footprints show how the
traveler detoured around messier parts of
the path. Even though the journey is more
challenging when the path is in this
condition, the footprints show that
someone went forward.

## Points to Ponder . . .

What do you remember about a time when you decided to keep
going, even though you knew the journey would be difficult?

What kept you going?

As a result of that experience, what changed within you that
would influence your actions in future circumstances?

How can you use what you have learned to make a difference in
the lives of people and organizations?

Important activity isn't always
visible on the surface.

# Inside Activity

After a spell of freezing rain, the sun is blessing the earth. A thick transparent sheet of ice covers a large boulder by the towpath. Although the late afternoon sun no longer touches the rock, its magical work continues. Under the ice, a drop of water forms, breaks free, and skitters down between ice and granite. As it joins with other small drops along the way, the flow gradually increases. Those few drops, working from the inside out, are wearing away winter's ice.

## Points to Ponder . . .

When have you been in a situation that felt like the movement of water between ice and granite? How did you handle it?

When is it best to work from the inside out?

What is happening in your life right now that would benefit from an inside-out approach?

No matter how out of control things seem to be,
there are still options.

# Options

A seasonal flood warning has been issued for the Potomac River. Near a lockhouse, a group of curiosity seekers and canal lovers gather on the towpath to watch the rapidly rising waters. As parts of the towpath are washed away, they sense personal danger, and feeling helpless, move to higher ground. A few miles upstream, a group working as a team, feverishly pile sandbags to protect their portion of the towpath.

*Points to Ponder . . .*

What image comes to mind when you think of an event over which you felt you had little or no control? What did you decide to do?

Looking back, how was your darkest hour also a time of possibility?

If someone asked you how this experience deepened your understanding of life, what would you say?

How can you use the insights from that experience as you deal with challenging transitions in organizational life? In family life? As you grow older?

In a classic power struggle,
no one really wins.

# Power Struggle

The leafless winter landscape reveals
a strong honeysuckle vine spiraling around
a small maple tree, tightening its grip as
the tree grows. In turn, the tree is changing
shape in response to the honeysuckle's
constraints. The steadily growing tree is
bulging out over the vine and gradually
enfolding it. Both are becoming distorted.

*Points to Ponder . . .*

How is a struggle between two strong forces — such as the
honeysuckle vine and the maple tree — represented in your
organization?

What are the underlying issues in this struggle — especially those
that aren't talked about?

What might happen if these issues were openly recognized and
talked about? What is likely to happen if everyone remains
silent?

What would need to happen to create a space for real dialogue
about these issues?

What first step could you take in that direction?

The promise of renewal is
sometimes found in unexpected
places and vulnerable constructions.

# Promise

As the westerly sun shines through
barren branches, pieces of thin brown paper
appear to be flapping in a late afternoon
breeze. Actually, a hornets' nest from last
summer — anchored to a twig and no
longer hidden by leaves — is beginning
to lose its outer layers. Although it appears
that the "paper palace" would crumble
at the slightest touch, the intricate
construction protects the young that
will emerge in the spring.

*Points to Ponder . . .*

What holds the promise of renewal in your life?

What protects this possibility?

What part does planning play? What part is happenstance?

In what ways has a bleak period in your life been a time of
personal growth? How were you changed as a result?

How do your personal experiences apply or not apply to the
change and renewal of organizations?

Taking time out clarifies the flow
of life's activities.

# Completing the Cycle

Observed through leafless trees from
high up on the towpath, a river channel
curves gently around a small island, away
from the main body of the river. In winter's
piercing cold, the water in the slow-moving
channel has become a clear blue-green. Silt
and other suspended material are now at
the river's bottom. Purified by its "time
out," the sparkling water rejoins the
mainstream in its journey on to the
Chesapeake Bay, the ocean, the clouds,
and then back again.

*Points to Ponder . . .*

What issues seem to get settled when you take time out from
daily life? What opportunities are available for doing that?

When, in your life, have you felt deep harmony with the natural
order of things?

How could you cultivate this state of being in every part of your
life?

How is it possible for an entire organization to maintain a clear,
easy-flowing state of being?